Sip & Solve

HARD CROSSWORDS

MATT GAFFNEY

Sterling Publishing Co., Inc.
New York

10 9 8 7 6 5 4 3 2 1

Published by Sterling Publishing Co., Inc.
387 Park Avenue South, New York, NY 10016
© 2005 by Gaffney Crossword Group, Inc.
Distributed in Canada by Sterling Publishing
c/o Canadian Manda Group, 165 Dufferin Street
Toronto, Ontario, Canada M6K 3H6
Distributed in Great Britain by Chrysalis Books Group PLC
The Chrysalis Building, Bramley Road, London W10 6SP, England
Distributed in Australia by Capricorn Link (Australia) Pty. Ltd.
P.O. Box 704, Windsor, NSW 2756, Australia

Sterling ISBN 1-4027-2988-X

For information about custom editions, special sales, premium and
corporate purchases, please contact Sterling Special Sales
Department at 800-805-5489 or specialsales@sterlingpub.com.

Contents

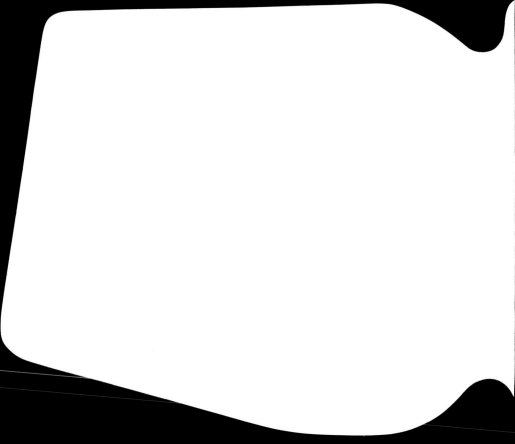

Introduction

The 42 crosswords in this book are small. Ergo, they must be easy to solve, right?

Not so! Lots of tough things come in small packages: diamond rings, featherweight boxers, stale beef jerky—and the crossword puzzles in this diminutive but demonically difficult volume. We've packed all the tricks and traps of a regular-size crossword into each one of these bite-size babies, so don't feel bad if they trip you up.

And if a kibitzer laughs, "What's wrong, you can't even solve a tiny crossword like that one?" just hand the book over with a smile. Your friend will be crying for a *Big 'n' Easy* crossword book in no time flat!

—Matt Gaffney

5

1

ACROSS

1 Prefix with cop
5 She had a *Tootsie* role
9 Corporation on season two of *The Apprentice*
10 Eddie of *Repo Man*
11 "Later days!"
13 It opened in 1899
14 "Whilst ___ home starve for a merry look": *The Comedy of Errors*
15 Presidential inits.
16 Half a Hawaiian dress
17 Places where decisions are made, for short
20 Becomes inaudible
22 Title address of a Paul Anka hit
24 *My Name* ___ (1998 movie about a Scottish alcoholic)
25 Salt River valley city
26 Wired ___ (powerful Texas hold'em cards)
27 Pompously inaccessible

DOWN

1 Character in many jokes
2 *Dafne* is considered the first
3 Muddle with liquor
4 Draft animals
5 Liguria's capital
6 Something in Spain
7 San Luis ___
8 Wu-Tang Clan rapper

Answer, page 90

10 Shortstop with nine Gold Gloves
12 Disbarred one
16 Posh home
17 Some craft do it
18 Trip with a point
19 Go wrong
20 Mountain an artist famously depicted 36 different ways
21 Psychotropic plant
22 Prairie dog's sound
23 Female bear: Spanish

7

2

ACROSS

1 Turkic language
7 City with over 100 mosques
10 "If I Can't Have You" singer Elliman
11 First name of a Hollywood great
12 King metioned in Proverbs
13 1970s–'80s new wave band Split ___
14 Señor's finale
15 Drink from the Russian word for "winter"
17 Pindar wrote about it
19 Molar holders
21 Basques fry them in oil
23 Discrepancies
25 Letters on Rome's coat of arms
27 Symbol of density
28 Peg game
30 *Mr. Belvedere* actor
32 Half a Thor Heyerdahl book
33 "Where are you?" reply
34 Naive utterance
35 Constellation near the Big Dipper

DOWN

1 First name in Aussie pop music
2 Ms. Mimieux
3 Architectural style
4 Stocky antelope
5 California's Santa ___ Mountains
6 Woody Allen character

Answer, page 90

7 Place to haggle
8 A as in Aachen
9 Dreamer's trio
16 Countenance, casually
18 Kleine Scheidegg, notably
20 The earth, e.g.
22 Short news item
24 Body blots
26 ___ *911!*
28 Witch
29 '50s prez
31 Actress/comic/ blogger

9

3

ACROSS

1 San Cristóbal de las ___, Mexico
6 "I ___ Man of Constant Sorrow"
9 Classic 1981 Genesis album
11 Cheesecake ingredient?
12 Random chorus
13 Santa ___, California
14 Cossack commander
16 Part of AMPAS
19 Lady, in León
20 Gardner and namesakes
21 *Enterprise* letters
22 Monkey meal
24 ___ standstill
25 Biblical haven
30 1987 album with five #1 hits
31 Costa del Sol city
32 Constellation near Centaurus
33 Highest national capital in the world

DOWN

1 Revered first name in Baltimore
2 Dr. J once played for it
3 ___ soda
4 Here, in Honduras
5 Tossed food
6 Long-tailed lizards
7 Capital on the Persian Gulf
8 Appliance brand
10 Try for a triple
15 Seat of Pontotoc County, Okla.

10

Answer, page 90

16 Online alter ego
17 Nunavut is part of it
18 Coca-Cola founder
   Candler
20 Part of an African
   capital
21 Pro-choice org.
23 Danielle Steel's
   Message From ___
26 Stylistically copying
27 Outkast's genre
28 Izmir honorific
29 Spinning cartoon
   character

11

4

ACROSS

1 Mock cry of wonder
7 ___ Pellegrino (bottled water brand)
10 Dental dreck
11 Award from HRH
12 Appeal in earnest
13 In the capacity of
14 Comment during a chess game indicating the piece being touched won't be moved
16 Kitchen strainer
19 Cambodian cash
20 About
21 Post-error offer from a computer
22 It gave aid to the indigent
24 Cooperstown's Galvin
25 Melodramatic goodbyes
29 Lash locale
30 Make the party interesting
31 Noted rock groupie Pamela ___ Barres
32 Word often seen in ads

DOWN

1 Grandpa, in Germany
2 Like some friends
3 Uris novel, with *The*
4 Visibly nervous
5 Atmospheres
6 Pay attention to
7 "I hate my job!" response
8 Druggie
9 How clothes may be folded

Answer, page 90

15 Two-time
Emmy-nominated
role

16 Prepared to solve, as
this book's title
suggests

17 Senator since '63

18 Undercuts

21 They start at the
center

23 Kabob component,
often

26 Attack a house,
prankster-style

27 Ending for vein

28 Gen-___

13

5

ACROSS
1 Arab League member
7 It might be checked
10 "That's right"
11 Federal case
12 Like some crystals
13 1982 Duran Duran album
14 Are, in Arles
15 Iraq War reporter
17 Julio's *hijo*
19 1600 Pennsylvania Avenue, e.g.
22 Knife that can cut aluminum cans!
23 Kind of tape
27 "Here Come the Warm Jets" musician
28 Went berserk
30 Washington ballplayer, for short
31 *Cocoon* Oscar winner
32 Article in *Time* magazine
33 Whip user

DOWN
1 Noted entrepreneur, or what he creates
2 Klinger's home
3 Hero of *Patriot Games*
4 Gordon of jazz et al.
5 1-800-___-HELP (number called on the roadside)
6 Avalanche, Hurricanes, and Lightning members
7 Chip flavor
8 Tearful "ta-ta"

Answer, page 90

14

9 "Johnny B. ___"
16 Botches
18 Of a bodily system
19 Cut taker
20 Shore who sure could sing
21 Scale part
24 Mark forever
25 "To ___ seems like diamond to glass": Shakespeare
26 European border river
29 "___ moron!"

15

6

ACROSS
1 Plzen person
6 Egyptian god
10 Ref
11 Take another stab at
12 Frijoles accompaniment
13 Baker in *The Godfather*
14 *60 Minutes* ponderer
16 Rose's home
17 Music stores may sell them
19 Include within a larger group
22 Weapon named for its inventor
23 #2, e.g.
27 Convert completer
29 Prop for many Westerns
30 Be a rat
31 Writer Calvino
32 Grey Goose rival
33 Classifies, in a way

DOWN
1 Drug ___
2 Total loser
3 River to the Mediterranean
4 Titan chief
5 Becomes cloudy
6 Post- antonym
7 Year in Augustus's reign
8 Like some wood that's been shaped
9 Sweatshirt parts
15 Riyal spenders

16

Answer, page 90

18 Mean
19 Higher-ups
20 Tashkent native
21 Beer of the 1970s
24 Draw (out)
25 Man, for example
26 Some summer
babies
28 Eponymous
1977 country album
Joe ___

17

7

ACROSS

1 Microsoft rival
7 Wine holder
10 High dozen
11 Sport ___
12 *Amadeus* and *The English Patient* producer Saul
13 Palindromic carb source
14 Troublemaker
15 Black ball
17 Considers
20 Model
24 San Diego State athlete
27 The Who's "Love Reign ___ Me"
28 "Wha?"
29 ___ with (equal to)
32 "Kudos"
33 "I'm serious!"
34 "Delish!"
35 Experiencing the munchies, e.g.

DOWN

1 1950s–'60s TV husband
2 Goes wherever
3 Skillful
4 The Reds, on scoreboards
5 Back muscle, for short
6 Scratching cause
7 *The Psychology of the Unconscious* author
8 Setting for the *Great Brain* book series
9 Chap
16 Way of looking at the world
18 Wide size

Answer, page 91

19 They're out now
21 Unannounced visit, on *Seinfeld*
22 Bolt
23 Went wrong
24 Word after "Chips"
25 Follower of X-ray and Yankee
26 Yonder folk
30 Meaning-inverting word
31 Garlic: Spanish

19

8

ACROSS
1 Modern music source
5 Org. created in 1914
10 Not a thing
11 Terra ___
12 Merle Haggard's "___ From Muskogee"
13 King bound to a spinning wheel, in Greek mythology
14 Hardly a quick learner
16 God, to some ancients
17 #1 hit of 1960 for Brenda Lee
19 Like some errors
22 Music sheet abbrs.
23 Gaudiness
27 Senator born in Montpelier
29 Jack's longtime boss on *Law & Order*
30 Kind of membranophone
31 One end of the Appian Way
32 Brazil's feijoada and Belgium's waterzooi
33 Go down, in a way

DOWN
1 Alligator brand
2 Toy dog, for short
3 Starbucks CEO Smith
4 "Can you really tell?"
5 Movie-lover's org.
6 A Washington and a Lincoln
7 Town ___
8 Love, in the Louvre

20

Answer, page 91

9 *Viola tricolor hortensis*, commonly
15 World's second-largest bird
18 Give in to gravity
19 Actor Peter et al.
20 "Mine eye and heart ___ a mortal war": Shakespeare
21 Dernier cri
24 *American ___*
25 Control
26 Adrian of *T.J. Hooker*
28 Rap shouts

21

9

ACROSS

1 Record company started by Russell Simmons
7 Computer program, for short
10 Social layers
11 Nidwalden neighbor
12 Casey's creator
13 Normal: Abbr.
14 "Take a hike!"
16 Get rid of duds
19 Part of town
20 It has a big spout
21 Target rival
22 Standard "attaboy"
24 Doo-___ music
25 First name in music
29 Actress Sue ___ Langdon
30 O'Neal title role of 1996
31 Eastern bread
32 Head-scratcher

DOWN

1 Sun-bringing letters
2 Ordinal suffix
3 Religious title
4 Paragon of nudity
5 Accepted uncritically
6 Munich month
7 Oscar-winning *Terms of Endearment* role for Shirley
8 Like better
9 Much of bacon
15 Victoria Falls' river

Answer, page 91

16 Alternative to walking

17 Countdown duo

18 Take up, as a cold case

21 It has 114 chapters

23 Swell

26 Price place

27 Ingredient in a croque-monsieur

28 Palindromic physicians' org.

23

10

ACROSS

1 TV's Warrior
 Princess et al.
6 Yahtzee category
10 Are
11 ___ Coast rap
12 Lexis-___
13 Contempt
 ending
14 "Am ___?" (queue
 query)
15 Console since
 2001
16 DDE beat him

17 Front
19 First cardinal of
 Cuba
20 Hippie's home
23 2001 Kevin Spacey
 movie
26 Trotsky, after
 1928
28 Damage
29 Bugs
30 Major map mass
31 *So I Married* ___
 Murderer
32 "Joyeux ___!"
33 Dr. Seuss story,
 with "The"

DOWN

1 Seat of Greene
 County, Ohio
2 Cervenka formerly
 of the rock band X
3 Gives the no-go
4 Battleship attempt
5 Common Polish
 church honoree,
 casually
6 In the middle of,
 cutesy-style
7 Spud that's not very
 large
8 It was destroyed by
 fire in 1624

Answer, page 91

9 "Babe" band
18 Of the same age
19 Famed Mayan ruin site
20 *Finding Nemo* animation studio
21 Billy Joel's "The Downeaster '___'"
22 Sterilize
23 Wrathful title character in a 1982 movie
24 Part of a Texas city
25 Music's India.___
27 Strange start?

25

11

ACROSS

1 "___ good at any thing, and yet a fool": *As You Like It*
6 Coors drink
10 Pee-wee travels to it in *Pee-wee's Big Adventure*
11 Birds: Latin
12 Strength
13 K.C. manager Tony
14 Rational finish
15 Forsake the arms of Morpheus
17 Bottoms in light
19 Mohandas, commonly
23 Certain peninsula-dweller
26 Cloth or bombard ending
27 Loser, according to anti-drug TV spots
28 Clemenza offs him in *The Godfather, Part II*
30 "Let's leave ___ that"
31 Ornamental bowl
32 Russian limousines
33 Eye problems

DOWN

1 Orthodox type
2 Early artificial intelligence program
3 Less cracked
4 Letters in some church names
5 It's hardly purse material
6 Hero in Chiapas
7 Poker champ Phil
8 Dessert ___
9 "Yesterday"

26

Answer, page 91

16 Some souvenirs

18 Blue light special locales

20 Whirl

21 Turkish tapas

22 Music drama's lack

23 Look for gaps in someone's knowledge

24 Moscato d'___ (Italian wine)

25 Color in 1980s new wave getups

29 "Ten thousand saw ___ a glance": Wordsworth

27

12

ACROSS

1 "Is it my turn?"
6 1925 Nobelist
10 Supreme Court chief justice, 1941–46
11 "Hold the Line" band
12 The people of Christchurch, e.g.
13 Marty Feldman role
14 Nev. neighbor
15 Game demand
17 Treaty city of 1842
19 Reduced dramatically
23 One of Cambridge's 31 colleges
26 Eggy combining form
27 DLX divided by V
28 Basketball commentator's phrase
30 Bonobos, e.g.
31 Certain eighth
32 Gym figures
33 Off-peak call?

DOWN

1 Invite to the foyer
2 Peak of Crete
3 Bettendorfer, e.g.
4 College, in Australian slang
5 In an irksome way
6 Fuzz operations
7 *Dukes of Hazzard* surname
8 Ubiquitous building block
9 Exhausted, with "out"
16 Senselessness

28

Answer, page 91

18 Nike rival
20 Took advantage of, in slang
21 Modern party announcement
22 ___ Logue of *The Tao of Steve*
23 It shouldn't be picked
24 Erstwhile ballplayer
25 Committed perjury
29 Poetic qualifier

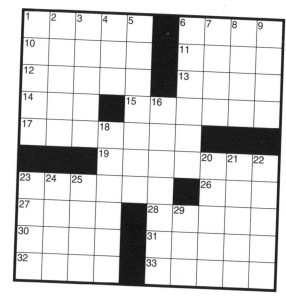

29

13

ACROSS
1 Citified area
4 Uninteresting
10 Kung ___ chicken
11 He was killed by melting wax
12 Kim Philby, notably
13 Role for Lorre
14 Narrow strip of land
16 Salinger title girl
17 Beats every time
21 "Only Time" singer
22 Promotion choice, usually
23 Classic film set in San Francisco
25 Except if
28 Lajoie of Cooperstown
29 Untouchable, in a way
30 *Année* quarter
31 Fake gold
32 ___ publica (the state)

DOWN
1 Expand
2 Strikes lightly, as a window
3 John, to Gabrielle, on *Desperate Housewives*
4 Pry open
5 Color that's French for "unbleached"
6 Really rocks
7 Logical prefix?
8 Devoted follower
9 Tijuana that
15 Dismissal
18 New York congressman Anthony
19 Offset

30

Answer, page 92

20 ___.com (popular myth-debunking site)
22 Post-P group
24 Class for immigrants
25 ___-Aztecan languages
26 Terence Trent D'Arby album *Neither Fish* ___ *Flesh*
27 Herbert of the Pink Panther movies

14

ACROSS
1 "Whatcha gonna do about it?"
6 "Forget it"
10 College class, casually
11 Pathetic
12 "Right!"
14 Jennings of *Jeopardy!*
15 Dos of a sort
16 Beat by a bit
19 Ranch alternative
23 Frank and others
26 Car name that's the initials of its creator
27 Mississippian beloved by Wisconsinites
30 Mitchell who did "Help Me"
31 *X-Files* extra
32 Lip ___
33 Four years before Tiberius became emperor of Rome

DOWN
1 Radius
2 Showed to seats, casually
3 Keeping a watch on
4 Year of Himmler's birth
5 Canadian tags
6 David-like wins
7 Time
8 *Cheers* shout
9 Buried treasures?
13 Running mate of presidential hopeful Bill the Cat
17 Like lingerie

32

Answer, page 92

18 Give the boot
20 Wide receiver Michael
21 Posta ___ (air mail, in Italy)
22 Perpetually
23 Sentence pts.
24 New York city
25 State that touches eight other states: Abbr.
28 Atkins Diet non-issue
29 Word on many microbreweries' bottles

33

15

ACROSS

1 Keep it cool
7 Kareem, in high school
10 French maid in the movie *Clue*
11 1961 hit song "___ Buttermilk Sky"
12 *Ocean's Twelve* actor
14 Short-lived 1980s sitcom ___ *Pablo*
15 Elevator sound
16 Gives an earful
19 Hallucinogenic cacti
23 Leningrad event
26 Underground vein
27 Feminists may subscribe to it
30 Einstein's birth city
31 It closes at night
32 It was once happy
33 Possessive on bags of candy

DOWN

1 In real life
2 Bring out
3 ___ dialysis
4 And so forth: Abbr.
5 Jock: Abbr.
6 A.L. RBI leader, 1976
7 City where Roman Polanski attended film school
8 2004 fantasy ___ *Enchanted*

34

Answer, page 92

9 Familiar
   fifty-secondth
13 Self-starter?
17 Org. for Se Ri Pak
18 Folk surname
20 Doesn't shirk
21 Tiger rival
22 Sesame and others
23 Arrogant
24 Menorca *o* Ibiza
25 Tube honor
28 Vote for
29 Tappan ___ Bridge

35

16

ACROSS
1 City built by Pachacuti
6 Clear malt drink
10 Take away
11 ___ Prairie, Minnesota
12 Concerning
14 Mini-___ (some submachine guns)
15 Agatha Christie's N ___?
16 Some speakers
18 Clock number
19 Mendes of *2 Fast 2 Furious*
20 Subtlety
22 ___ loss
23 Pacific short-finned ___
24 Didn't throw in the towel
28 "You're putting ___!"
29 Martha Graham's field
30 Await judgment
31 "Bye!"

DOWN
1 No purebred
2 Exercise
3 Shaka founded it
4 1961 country crossover hit
5 Claimed dibs on, as a novel
6 Spiritually deep
7 "How on earth do you manage?"

36

Answer, page 92

8 Way of measuring
9 Societal purposelessness
13 Campaign season staples
16 Lampooned
17 Reluctant
21 Pool problem
25 Point
26 Not real social
27 Largest union in the U.S.

37

17

ACROSS
1 Put down
4 1983 finalist at Wimbledon
10 One of two three-letter movies ever nominated for Best Picture
11 Part of L.A.
12 Ecclesiastes phrase
14 They get checks for checking
15 Holiday money
16 River named by La Salle
21 Beginning
23 A little power
24 License datum
26 Latex source
30 *The Birdcage* actor
31 Blow it
32 They're barred from bars
33 MIT undergrad degrees

DOWN
1 First name in jazz guitarists
2 Kind of statement
3 Know-how
4 Give the ol' raspberry to
5 With jangled nerves
6 Prefix with type
7 WWII fighters
8 Co-producer of U2's *The Joshua Tree*
9 Scuffle
13 Give (out)
17 "Or else ___ by folly vanquished": *The Two Gentlemen of Verona*

38

Answer, page 92

18 Tomislav Square's city
19 Everybody else
20 Sea ___ (fur sources)
22 English 101 word
25 Bullpen stats
26 Zodiac creature
27 Weapon first used in battle in 1956
28 Criminalize
29 Chum

39

18

ACROSS
1 Trudge
5 Where one can get a little Lamb?
10 It's between James and Jones
11 Word on Scarlett letters?
12 Movie taglined "Change the way you look at the world"
13 Anne Tyler novel *Searching for* ___
14 1999 Ron Howard film
15 City east of L.A.
16 Like lousy chicken soup
18 Get, as grifters
19 Taper?
21 Got rid of
23 Member of *Pan troglodytes*, familiarly
25 Skeleton key?
28 Part of a magic word
29 Virgin ___
30 More than miffed
31 Divination topic
32 Trapper's stock
33 Five-time Best Actor nominee

DOWN
1 Chinese barker
2 *Dragnet* gp.
3 Talky, so to speak
4 566
5 Triangular bone
6 Word in 1979 headlines
7 "Emily Lime" is one
8 Combat location

Answer, page 92

40

9 Important person
17 Tiredness causes them
19 Program monitor
20 Dishes, e.g.
22 Private investigator, frequently
24 Crossbreed
26 Sean's costar in *The Hunt for Red October*
27 'merican

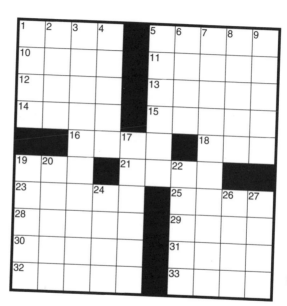

41

19

ACROSS

1 World capital since 1991
6 Goalie gear
10 No big spender
11 First name in bassi
12 Up in the air
13 Martin of *Sabrina, the Teenage Witch*
14 1968 nominee for Best Director
16 Hockey player Tikkanen
17 Word heard in Boston and Chicago
18 *The Federalist Papers* co-author
19 Tent-pitching org.
22 Group of six
26 "This guy walks into ___ ..."
27 Uncovered
28 Bamboozle
29 Best
30 Court opener
31 Bree ___ Kamp (*Desperate Housewives* role)

DOWN

1 Thrill
2 Some humours
3 From sea to shining sea, cutesy-style
4 Bridges in California
5 Guild member, perhaps
6 South-of-the-border gas station
7 Blue: Spanish
8 Borscht flavoring, often
9 Passages for one person
15 Colorful character?

Answer, page 93

42

18 Spanish town after which sherry wine is named

19 One of George's advisers

20 First non-B.C. year

21 Confuse

22 It added seven members in 2004

23 Company whose second letter is capitalized

24 ACC team, for short

25 Terhune's ___ *Dog*

43

20

ACROSS
1 ___ straight face (didn't smile)
6 Roc-a-Fella Records co-founder
10 A little truth
11 First name of two Nobel Peace Prize winners
12 *Training Day* director
13 "Uh-uh"
14 Feature of fumblers
16 Green Day song "Words I Might Have ___"
17 Kid in jazz
18 Official carrier of Tokyo Disney
19 Calendar abbr.
22 It reads the same across and down
26 Close to closed
27 Contraction in some questions
28 Put on
29 It may be golden: Abbr.
30 With all due speed
31 Late ABC exec Arledge

DOWN
1 *In Der Strafkolonie* author
2 Be jubilant
3 Arouse
4 Praise
5 Large ladies
6 Jones or McCarthy
7 Eczema battler
8 Putting problem, with "the"

44

Answer, page 93

9 Sequence finishers
15 Bush Doctrine test
18 Spot seller
19 Indicate
  unwillingness
20 Senator in
  Watergate headlines
21 Bother
22 Baba ___ (*SNL*
  sketch figure)
23 Lima lookers
24 Like many an avis
25 "I think I'll pass,
  actually"

ACROSS

1 Inventor who worked for a time with Edison
6 Flow blockers
10 Storage space
11 Shakira song "Estoy ___"
12 Brownish hue
13 Total jerk
14 Relaxed
15 6/6/44, e.g.
16 Asthmatic's device
18 Merger hope
22 Small quantity
25 Country name from 1971 to 1997
26 Signing gorilla
27 Where some work out
28 Holy image: Var.
29 Lee beater
30 Toy breed, casually
31 Sea birds

DOWN

1 *The Green Berets* actor
2 Joel's brother
3 Secret supply
4 One way to sink
5 How sarcastic remarks may be made
6 Head-in-the-clouds type
7 ___ pura
8 Alley wanderer

46

Answer, page 93

9 Tag info
17 Reaction starter
19 Costa ___
20 D, say
21 Salesman's goals
22 Uno card
23 Grab the attention
of, in a way
24 "Fine, sheesh!"

47

22

ACROSS
1 Made clucking sounds
6 Piece variety
10 Barbera's cartoon partner
11 Thumbs-down
12 Useless
13 Logician's word
14 Is totally shocked
15 Toffee bar
16 Mulberry Street's creator
18 Good way to saute mushrooms
22 Senator in space, 1985
25 First month, to some
26 Scope
27 Construct
28 Tongue heard in New Mexico
29 Make eggs, maybe
30 Francisco's affection
31 Provence city

DOWN
1 Bronze
2 Less whacked-out
3 Assaults, in a way
4 Outside
5 Make until 1983
6 Older than a given person
7 Budget bloater
8 Fought-over food

48

Answer, page 93

9 Way out
17 K2 guide
19 ___ Beagle (noted TV bar)
20 Funnyman Vilanch
21 Freshman may look up to them
22 City taken by Crusaders
23 ___ lily
24 She ordered González back to Cuba

49

23

ACROSS
1 ___ stick
5 Rewards Card offerer
10 Play opening
11 "Obviously!"
12 Party mix component
13 *Rent* or *Tommy*, e.g.
14 Word from the Chinese for "bump head"
16 Give one star to
17 Aim for a pin
19 Like some sexy voices
22 Dunking Ming
23 Kind of glasses
27 Big discovery of 1930
29 Plotting
30 "Imperial March" composer
31 ___-up (confined)
32 Blue Moon, and others
33 "I guess"

DOWN
1 Zippo
2 Calle ___ (Little Havana draw)
3 Carbonnade, e.g.
4 Somewhat tallish, for a man
5 "For the Lord ___ the way of the righteous": Psalms
6 Take on a spill
7 Sure-handed
8 Country
9 ___ of Glamis (Macbeth)

50

Answer, page 93

15 Twain and Dickens, notably
18 Too sentimental
19 One who likes to chill out
20 Winner of an Oscar the same year as Denzel
21 Cheek cover
24 Foil cousin
25 "Is to the foot of thund'ring ___ joined": Virgil
26 Performs, biblically
28 Viscous liquid

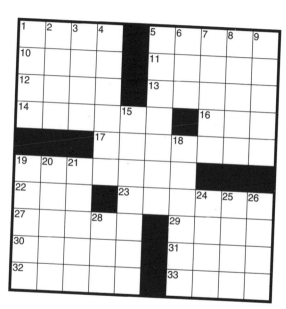

51

24

ACROSS

1 19-across was one
6 Boris Godunov, e.g.
10 Infomercial company
11 Take on
12 Open a case, maybe
13 Grinds (out)
14 Anti-pot org.
15 "Huh?"
17 Break performer
19 *The Prizefighter and the Lady* actor
23 Friendly neighbor, to Americans
26 ___ Schunk (Jesse Ventura's lieutenant governor)
27 1980 Boston Marathon cheater
28 Serious
30 It left from Iolcos
31 Emanated
32 Auto finish
33 Down and out

DOWN

1 Oil classification
2 Makes keen
3 Gallipoli fighter, for short
4 ___ Center (D.C. arena)
5 Traffic cause
6 Cyberspace
7 Punjabi, probably
8 Part of the city
9 Put one's feet up
16 France's shape, roughly

52

Answer, page 93

18 Belem's banks
20 Impress mightily
21 Like some roofs
22 Like the sound of a sax
23 Symbol of Maryland
24 Glow
25 Close
29 Richard ___ (unidentified male, in court)

25

ACROSS
1 "No sweat"
6 Person who's seen the Ka'aba
10 ___-Maritime (department of northern France)
11 "This place is ___!"
12 Comintern founder
13 Word spoken many times by Robin Williams
14 And more: Abbr.
15 Leipzig-born composer
17 1997 Michael Douglas thriller
19 Product with simple directions
23 "No more for me"
26 Law man
27 *Desperate Housewives* actress Hatcher
28 Weed
30 Word that's often illuminated
31 Used, as plates
32 Planes seen in *Top Gun*
33 Bloody ruler

DOWN
1 Land in the water
2 Enforcement power
3 Because
4 "Don't Blame It ___" (reggae song)
5 *Wiseguy* star
6 Phrase heard in Westerns
7 Minaret summons

54

Answer, page 94

8 Completed
9 *Semaine* part
16 Blend
18 Blackout preventers
20 To put, in Peru
21 Sarcastic "I'm so excited about that"
22 One of about three million
23 Thing
24 Taco Bell prefix
25 Kitchen appliance, for short
29 One ___ time

55

26

ACROSS
1 Rabanne of fashion
5 Not seriously
10 Lomi salmon is eaten during it
11 *Chasing the Dream* autobiographer
12 Only a few people can get it
14 Hellenic H
15 Ready for action
16 Bible pts.
18 McDermid and Kilmer
19 Country that anagrams into a world capital
21 Favored
22 "The Land of the Midnight Sun"
24 Wagering letters
27 Colorado senator
29 Microsoft product
30 Peacekeepers for over 1,000 generations
31 Let live
32 First name of two of the Beastie Boys

DOWN
1 It requires the knees to bend
2 Grandpa's daughter, possibly
3 City on the Atlantic
4 Not non
5 Road that leads to Rome
6 "Really!"
7 Australian gamut
8 Jaleel White role
9 Relationship discussion topic
13 4–6–3 and 5–4–3, in baseball stats

56

Answer, page 94

17 Puss
19 Brings home
20 ___ Keaton (TV role)
21 Mac
23 Iron source
25 "Et voilà!"
26 Overflow (with)
28 Palindromic 1977 album

57

27

ACROSS

1 Institute for libertarians
5 Amount of cookies
10 "Despite that," online
11 Earthy tone
12 An eagle gnawed at his liver
14 Chatter
15 ___ *Waldo?*
16 1961 Jerry Butler hit "___ Telling You"
18 Tie out West
19 Departed
21 "Yo!"
22 "We've received permission to begin"
24 Shirley Temple Black, to Ghana in the 1970s: Abbr.
27 Coca-Cola product
29 Good way to saute garlic
30 Candy bar that was featured prominently in a *Seinfeld* episode
31 Hauled off
32 Glamorously exciting

DOWN

1 "Roger"
2 Brand since 1977
3 Didn't rush things
4 Physicist Georg
5 Neither opposite
6 *Things Fall Apart* author
7 Pretentious pronoun
8 Eighth Amendment word
9 "___ Fine"

Answer, page 94

58

13 Women's pool champ ___ Laurance

17 ___ bread (South African dish)

19 Cap

20 "... ___'clock scholar"

21 Today, in Taxco

23 Gym founder Joe

25 1059

26 Like Toyota's Scion xB

28 Uranians, e.g.

59

28

ACROSS
1 Fattens the pigs
6 Blubber
10 Book whose name means "salvation"
11 Queens stadium
12 It warns against "carb blowouts"
14 Pres. Mbeki's land
15 Calls up
16 When Michael Corleone dies
18 Football players' wear
22 Corner store
25 Goddess: Latin
26 "Is that a fact?"
28 Pound in the stacks
29 Krispy ___
30 Baseball feature
31 ___ nothing

DOWN
1 Like some cheese
2 Word before luck
3 Expressionist artist Kokoschka
4 Part of Can.
5 Home port of the *USS Ronald Reagan*
6 Miss reason
7 "Right!"
8 Sharpen
9 Court calls
13 Jaffna's land
17 REO Speedwagon's "Down by ___"
19 Ranger or Villager
20 "I love you," to some

60

Answer, page 94

21 Leo with two #1 hits in the 1970s
22 Rounds you can sleep through
23 Give off
24 ___ mater (brain part)
27 MTV show

61

29

ACROSS
1 Aircraft carrier launched in 1976
7 Uris title word
10 1968 R&B album ___ *Now*
11 Prefix with terrorist
12 Becomes the buddy of
14 Name trademarked in 1899
15 *Hill Street Blues* actor
18 Vanya's creator
19 Single chance
21 PlayStation 2 maker
22 Chi-town paper
24 Pranksters pull them
28 State sch. in Kingston
29 Loud insect
30 Mormons: Abbr.
31 "Here"

DOWN
1 Nod off
2 Funds for later
3 Key West's ___ Fisher Maritime Museum
4 "See you then!"
5 So
6 *Weasels Ripped My Flesh* guitarist
7 Slated for possession of, as a fortune
8 Blockbuster section
9 Cash in black
13 Reconquers
15 Busker's take

Answer, page 94

16 Partner's share, maybe

17 Mediterranean plant named for its land of origin

20 Plot

23 Skater Kulik

25 Sally Field title word

26 Nine years after Columbus first crossed the Atlantic

27 Took a stool sample?

63

30

ACROSS
1 Russian submarine that sank in 2000
6 Lose it
10 Palindromic senator
11 Noted cotton exporter
12 Members of the 1992 world champion cricket team
14 Expend
15 Jai alai ball
16 "Search and Destroy" political cartoonist
18 "You win," poshly
22 Best in the ring
25 Bearing
26 *The Firebird* composer
28 Command to a canine
29 Places for breakfast
30 Wasn't creative
31 "Hit the gas!"

DOWN
1 Useless
2 Command from higher up
3 Left no leaves
4 Go downhill fast
5 Noted proponent of the Gruenfeld Defense
6 Starting to like?
7 Prefix with second
8 Got off
9 Italian university city
13 Communicating with, obsoletely

Answer, page 94

64

17 Vulgar but funny
19 CNN exec Jordan who resigned in 2005
20 Prince's "Darling ___"
21 Exciting appointment
22 Govt. arm since 1971
23 Coll. near the Mexican border
24 Corner
27 "___-Turn"

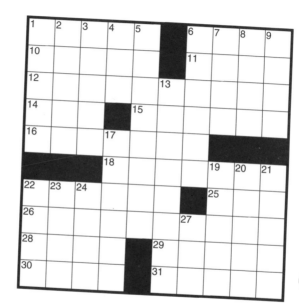

65

31

ACROSS
1 Optimist's phrase
5 Gin gulps
10 Add up (to)
11 It's digested in portions
12 1961 movie costarring Angela Lansbury
14 Its capital is Fort-de-France
15 Rock variety
16 Poet Plato called "the tenth Muse"
20 State coffers
25 "Olé!"
26 ___-Gavras (Z director)
27 Goes for the gold
28 Mr. Kringle
29 Lots of money

DOWN
1 SALT issue
2 Diet ___
3 River the Chinese call Heilongjiang
4 Noted depilatory
5 Tinny, so to speak
6 Maui ___ (pot variety)
7 Part of OIF
8 Common praenomen
9 Turns (away from)
13 Where Neptune rules
16 Catch on
17 Mail, for instance

Answer, page 95

18 Britney has pitched it
19 Splits
21 French foursome
22 Numeral on some clocks
23 First name in daredeviltry
24 Mobutu ___ Seko (Zairian dictator)

1	2	3	4		5	6	7	8	9
10					11				
12				13					
14									
				15					
16	17	18	19						
20						21	22	23	24
25									
26						27			
28						29			

67

32

ACROSS
1 "Do I have to draw you ___?"
5 They might fly in bars
10 ___ Park, N.Y.
11 It depends on how you look at it
12 Da capo
13 Certain Summer Olympian
14 Gary played him in *Immortal Beloved*
16 General of chicken fame
17 "Like, wow!"
19 A Flock of Seagulls' genre
22 Body spray with sexy ads
23 Like about 2% of Americans
27 Start of Caesar's boast
29 Word in the lyrics to "Rudolph the Red-Nosed Reindeer"
30 Term of affection
31 Anonymous Mr. Smithee
32 Tough guy to trust
33 Makes number one?

DOWN
1 Great salt lake
2 Offered food
3 Seniors, with "the"
4 Conference
5 Cancel
6 Google's was in 2004
7 Took care of

68

Answer, page 95

8 Lock
9 Noted Detroit brewer
15 "Sorry, that was obnoxious of me"
18 Tchotchke
19 Imitates perfectly
20 One who used to be in
21 Bob's go-with
24 That: Latin
25 County city
26 She-lobsters
28 Edwin McCain's "Write ___ Song"

69

33

ACROSS
1 Huddle shout
6 More, in Munich
10 Building game
11 Award first given in 1959
12 Small vases, e.g.
14 ___ Motor Car Co. Ltd.
15 Language spoken in Oaxaca
16 Group with the 1985 hit "I Miss You"
18 Like many protesters
22 Slivovitz, for instance
25 Bank deposit?
26 He was a little loco
28 Moises in the outfield
29 Three-dimensional figure
30 Oppression, metaphorically
31 Washes (off)

DOWN
1 Former member of the Sugarcubes
2 Turn
3 "Bon appétit!"
4 Space or Stone
5 Cat Stevens classic
6 1421
7 Israeli port
8 Charter

Answer, page 95

9 Org. for armed seniors
13 Past middle age
17 Would-be
19 Angora and cashmere
20 Clarinetist Shaw
21 Swamp things
22 Party time, casually
23 Candy rack cylinder
24 Had ___ time (sort of enjoyed oneself)
27 Losing tic-tac-toe line

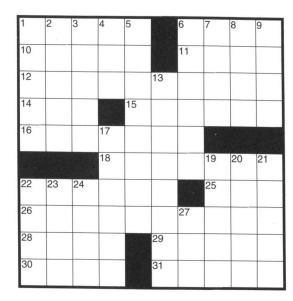

71

34

ACROSS
1 Let go
7 Like the *Queer Eye* guys
10 Former infantryman
11 Hoppy quaff
12 Jack's feature, maybe
13 Stern's org.
14 Winning sign
15 First name of a young Oscar winner
17 Icebreaker, often
20 No places for vinyl
22 Surname for "Jenny From the Block"
23 Signing stuff
26 ___ roll
27 Enormous flower of South America
30 Left and up a little: Abbr.
31 Go back (on)
32 Palindromic appellation
33 Bulls get excited when it goes up

DOWN
1 Sea of ___
2 Word with waffle or sugar
3 1. d4 mover
4 Gulf nat.
5 Columbia, e.g.
6 Be on the brink
7 Had daydreams
8 1976's *2112*, for one
9 Former New York City mayor
16 Secret number, often

72

Answer, page 95

18 Gobbled up
19 Noted member of the Freemasons
20 Horror film character, often
21 Summer of songs
24 "Fuggedaboutit"
25 Had the scoop
28 "I don't care either way"
29 "I'd like to buy ___"

73

35

ACROSS
1 "Shut yer ___!"
4 Certain key
10 "___ believe in yesterday ..."
11 King of England, Denmark, and Norway
12 Fictional character who wears an eyepatch
14 Let one's attention lapse, with "out"
15 Attention-getters
16 Totally uncool type
18 Go (through)
20 Court backup
22 HST, e.g.
23 Suffix with form
24 Pitts of *No, No, Nanette*
26 "Les Fleurs du Mal" poet
30 French or German
31 Top, for one
32 Taken care of
33 Word for a ship

DOWN
1 Rude youth, in England
2 "Caught you!"
3 Some places put sugar in it
4 Friedman's field, for short
5 Producer
6 *Bolero* actress Obregón
7 Theater buy
8 *Becket* actor
9 Possessive with Pieces

74

Answer, page 95

13 Move slowly
16 Goes diving
17 Blenheim, notably
19 Res ___ loquitur
21 1937 Medicine
Nobelist Albert
___-Gyorgyi
25 ___ trombone
27 Thieves' place
28 South Korea's
president, 1988–93
29 Watch

75

36

ACROSS
1 One of Alaska's two
6 Grandmas, in Garmisch-Partenkirchen
10 Distant
11 Enthusiastic agreement from Helmut
12 Home to a unique species of seal
14 Alternative to *du*
15 Curved weaponry
16 ___ acetate
18 Pitying sounds
19 Fight scene sound
21 Soccer squad based in Amsterdam
24 *My Michael* novelist
27 *Giants in the Earth* author Rolvaag
28 One performing a strutting dance
30 Flames that went out
31 "___ evil"
32 Casual greeting
33 Make androgynous

DOWN
1 Style of music that's also a food
2 Say
3 Dance with directions
4 Heartache
5 Altus, Ellsworth, et al.
6 Only tribe to defeat the Sioux
7 Lightens the mood
8 Permitting limited access
9 *Do the Right Thing* pizzeria

76

Answer, page 95

13 One step below "The Show"

17 ___ step (falls behind)

20 "I'm speechless"

22 Coeur d'___

23 Company associated with Rochester, N.Y.

24 Banda ___ (city in Indonesia devastated by 2004's tsunami)

25 Priest in reggae

26 Gale's costar on *The Gale Storm Show*

29 Cariou of *About Schmidt*

37

ACROSS
1 First letter in Greece
6 Where Scipio defeated Hannibal
10 Bayer brand
11 One who's two ago
12 Early Beatles tune "___ Is"
13 Took
14 Rapper with a fictional advanced degree
15 Nice cuts
17 "Where do we go from here?"
19 Poker variant where the pot is split
23 Omsk's river
26 Actress Plumb
27 Turn the other cheek?
28 Where Americans aren't Yankees
30 Doing
31 Ramones tune "Judy Is ___"
32 Younger sibling, at times
33 Nurse's concerns

DOWN
1 Favorite of the Eszterhazy family
2 ___ GX
3 Put back on, as a patch
4 Sixth-century date
5 "You're gonna love what I have to say"
6 Before first
7 Nerve cell part
8 Early Iranian
9 Plural of a two-, a three-, and a four-letter word

78

Answer, page 96

16 Tamerlane conquest of 1401
18 "I guess so"
20 Toyota brand
21 Like baaing
22 Septuple groups
23 "My turn"
24 Hitchcock film that takes place entirely in a single apartment
25 Kids
29 It sends some stocks soaring: Abbr.

79

38

ACROSS
1 Spinnaker supporters
6 Currency in Colombia
10 Jabbok River city
11 Fires
12 Yosa Buson's art
13 Battleship guess
14 New Mexico's ___ National Monument
16 Bk. of the Bible
17 *Star Trek* role for Montalban
18 Urban clothing line
20 *Today* rival, initially
23 UCLA's student newspaper, with *The*
26 Zebus, e.g.
27 With ___ of (vaguely tasting like)
28 Pronoun for a señorita
29 View anew
30 Champs of 1975 and 1976
31 Former NFL placekickers Matt and Chris

DOWN
1 *The Influence of Sea Power Upon History* author
2 Blow away
3 Big name in ham
4 Cut
5 Passed cleverly

80

Answer, page 96

6 Palazzo della Ragione location
7 Put out
8 Ensured, with "up"
9 Bogotá bears
15 Pie plant
19 They parallel radiuses
21 Molly Maguire, occupationally
22 Wants in
23 Evil ending
24 Supporting shaft
25 Daughter of Uranus

81

39

ACROSS
1 Rebekah's brother, mentioned in Genesis
6 .bmp alternative
10 Get by
11 ___-B (toothbrush brand)
12 Noted shopping district
13 Tourist's need, perhaps
14 In need of aphrodisiacs
16 Watch dogs
17 Contract
22 It's often served with figs
26 1989 comedy ___ the Viking
27 Children's author Sachar
28 It marked its 800th anniversary in 2001
29 Kick out
30 One to one, e.g.
31 Nakskov natives

DOWN
1 Edge
2 Foo Fighters song "Walkin' ___"
3 Cake choice
4 Splitting tools
5 Drawing close
6 God of the heavens
7 ___ fixe
8 Antonym for "tauten"

82

Answer, page 96

9 Bag brand
15 Wouldn't go
18 Spanish wine, or its region
19 City whose cathedral was painted by Monet
20 For later
21 Adam et al.
22 Naught
23 Hardly temperate
24 Dallas's nickname, with "the"
25 Crooks' letters

83

40

ACROSS
1 Very little
5 "Like ___!"
10 Copter relative
11 Goes berserk
12 Auburn and black, for two
14 Bezos business
15 Inquisition figure Bernardo ___
16 Single person
18 64-card game
21 "Thriller" video costar ___ Ray
22 Makes less dangerous
26 Lime cousin
28 Some MoMA pieces
29 Lat., Lith., et al.
30 Spot in the Bible
31 Vinegary shreds

DOWN
1 Turkish title of respect
2 Geom. calculation
3 Battle song?
4 Dog also called the Russian wolfhound
5 Polio treatment, once
6 Commentator Thomas
7 Quick and lively
8 Fred Berry role
9 ___ Mae Williams (Strom Thurmond's once-secret daughter)

84

Answer, page 96

13 Norman stormin',
with "the"
17 Pines
18 Big bangs
19 Julia Louis-Dreyfus
role of 2002–03
20 Word not on new
maps
23 Echt
24 Transcending: Prefix
25 Bush cabinet
member
27 Part of a smart
woman's name

41

ACROSS
1 Transylvania weapon
6 Hawk
10 1992 title role for Nicholson
11 Princess ___ Organa
12 *Mask* actor
14 Folkie Williams
15 Like some bread
16 Lookout Mountain general
18 Bugs
22 Ford model
25 Clock setting: Abbr.
26 1983 Wynton Marsalis album
28 Western city
29 Bony, in a way
30 Sets a price of
31 Piece of armor

DOWN
1 Gets rid of
2 Literally, "law"
3 Lit
4 Colonel's letters
5 Con target
6 Former GM chairman Alfred et al.
7 Japanese delicacies unagi and anago, for two
8 *Finding Myself* author Toby
9 Hardly hard-working
13 Evoke with finesse
17 They're thick-skinned

86

Answer, page 96

19 Russell and Kass
20 Best and others
21 Cubic meter
22 Brand in the
   bathroom
23 Women
24 Colorfully named
   pop star
27 Popular peninsula:
   Abbr.

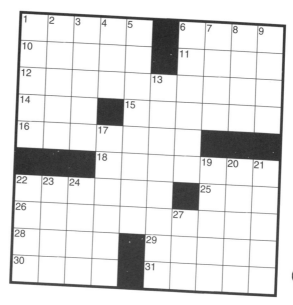

87

42

ACROSS
1 Emmy winner of 1980 and 1982
5 Whence Queen Amidala
10 Head of the Sorbonne
11 Reach rival
12 Besides
13 Makes (one's way)
14 1992 Disney offering
16 Mr. Chaney

17 Six in a row
21 Chicago suburb
23 Bethesda org.
24 Mean
26 Hard stuff
29 Color in stanzas
30 Alternative to Bradford or Bosc
31 Emmy winner of 1974, 1977, 1979, and 1982
32 Source of the phrase "wolf in sheep's clothing"
33 Liver, e.g.

DOWN
1 Takes third, say
2 "Fine, then"
3 "___-brainer!"
4 Drove, with "off"
5 "Understood"
6 Fail to be
7 Secret alternative
8 Former
9 No longer used: Abbr.
15 Force to increase
18 Lacking the skills

88

Answer, page 96

19 Tessio's portrayer
20 "___ a loss in how to go on when speaking, cough" (Greek proverb)
22 Easy instrument
25 Set of 500
26 Shearing sound
27 United
28 Breakfast orders

89

1

R	O	B	O				G	A	R	R
A	P	E	X			V	E	L	E	Z
B	E	S	E	E	I	N	G	Y	A	
B	R	O	N	X	Z	O	O			
I	A	T		J	Q	A				
		M	U	U		H	Q	S		
	F	A	D	E	S	O	U	T		
Y	O	U	N	G	L	O	V	E	R	
I	S	J	O	E		M	E	S	A	
P	A	I	R			A	R	T	Y	

2

K	Y	R	G	Y	Z		F	E	Z
Y	V	O	N	N	E		L	I	Z
L	E	M	U	E	L		E	N	Z
I	T	A		Z	I	M	A		
E	T	N	A		G	U	M	S	
	E	E	L	S		G	A	P	S
	S	P	Q	R		R	H	O	
H	I	Q		U	E	C	K	E	R
A	K	U		I	N	H	E	R	E
G	E	E		B	O	O	T	E	S

3

C	A	S	A	S		A	M	A
A	B	A	C	A	B		G	A	M
L	A	L	A	L	A		A	N	A
		A	T	A	M	A	N		
	A	C	A	D		D	A	M	A
A	V	A	S		N	A	S	A	
B	A	N	A	N	A				
A	T	A		A	R	A	R	A	T
B	A	D		M	A	L	A	G	A
A	R	A		L	A	P	A	Z	

4

O	O	H	A	A	H		S	A	N
P	L	A	Q	U	E		O	B	E
A	D	J	U	R	E		Q	U	A
		I	A	D	J	U	S	T	
S	I	E	V	E		R	I	E	L
I	N	R	E		R	E	T	R	Y
P	O	O	R	L	A	W			
P	U	D		A	D	I	E	U	X
E	Y	E		M	I	N	G	L	E
D	E	S		B	I	G	G	E	R

5

J	O	R	D	A	N		B	A	G
O	H	Y	E	A	H		A	D	O
B	I	A	X	A	L		R	I	O
S	O	N	T		E	M	B	E	D
		E	N	R	I	Q	U	E	
A	D	D	R	E	S	S			
G	I	N	S	U		D	E	M	O
E	N	O		R	I	O	T	E	D
N	A	T		A	M	E	C	H	E
T	H	E		L	A	S	H	E	R

6

C	Z	E	C	H		P	T	A	H
Z	E	B	R	A		R	E	D	O
A	R	R	O	Z		E	N	Z	O
R	O	O	N	E	Y		B	E	D
		U	S	E	D	C	D	S	
S	U	B	S	U	M	E			
U	Z	I		P	E	N	C	I	L
I	B	L	E		N	O	O	S	E
T	E	L	L		I	T	A	L	O
S	K	Y	Y		S	E	X	E	S

7

```
O R A C L E   J U G
Z O D I A C   U T E
Z A E N T Z   N A N
I M P     E I G H T
E S T E E M S
      E X A M P L E
A Z T E C   O E R
H U H   O N A P A R
O L E   N O J I V E
Y U M   S T O N E D
```

8

```
I P O D   A S C A P
Z E R O   F I R M A
O K I E   I X I O N
D E N S E   D E U S
      I M S O R R Y
F A C T U A L
A R R S   G L I T Z
L E A H Y   A D A M
K A Z O O   R O M E
S T E W S   S L E D
```

9

```
D E F J A M   A P P
S T R A T A   U R I
T H A Y E R   R E G
      B U Z Z O F F
S T R I P   A R E A
E W E R   K M A R T
G O O D J O B
W O P   A R E T H A
A N E   K A Z A A M
Y E N   E N I G M A
```

10

```
X E N A S   T W O S
E X I S T   W E S T
N E X I S   I B L Y
I N E X T   X B O X
A E S   A C T
      U N O   P A D
K P A X   E X I L E
H A R M   V E X E S
A S I A   A N A X E
N O E L   L O R A X
```

11

```
H E S A S   Z I M A
A L A M O   A V E S
S I N E W   P E N A
I Z E   S T A Y U P
D A R K E S T
      M A H A T M A
Q A T A R I   I E R
U S E R   R I Z Z I
I T A T   T A Z Z A
Z I L S   S T Y E S
```

12

```
A M I U P   S H A W
S T O N E   T O T O
K I W I S   I G O R
I D A   K I N G M E
N A N K I N G
      S L A S H E D
S E L W Y N   O V O
C X I I   I T S I N
A P E S   T H E T A
B O D S   Y O D E L
```

13

```
URB  JEJUNE
PAO  ICARUS
SPY  MRMOTO
ISTHMUS
ZOOEY  OWNS
ENYA  QUEEN
  VERTIGO
UNLESS NAP
TOOHOT ETE
ORMOLU RES
```

14

```
SUEME  UHNO
PSYCH  POOR
OHIMSOSURE
KEN  PERMS
EDGEOUT
  RUSSIAN
OTTOS  REO
BRETTFAVRE
JONI  ALIEN
SYNC  TENAD
```

15

```
BEREAL  LEW
YVETTE  OLE
DONCHEADLE
AKA  MUZAK
YELLSAT
  PEYOTES
SIEGE  ORE
MSMAGAZINE
ULM  EYELID
GAY  REESES
```

16

```
CUZCO  ZIMA
USURP  EDEN
RELATINGTO
 UZIS  ORM
SANYOS  III
EVA  NUANCE
NET  EELS
TRIEDAGAIN
USON  DANCE
PEND  SEEYA
```

17

```
DIS  JAEGER
JFK  ENCINO
ATIMETOSOW
NHLERS
GELT  YAZOO
ONSET  WATT
  HEIGHT
RUBBERTREE
AZARIA  ERR
MINORS  BSS
```

18

```
PLOD  CSPAN
EARL  OHARA
KPAX  CALEB
EDTV  CHINO
 OILY  NAB
VCR  AXED
CHIMP  XRAY
HOCUS  COLA
IRATE  OMEN
PELTS  PECK
```

19

A	B	U	J	A		P	A	D	S
M	I	S	E	R		E	Z	I	O
A	L	O	F	T		M	U	L	L
Z	E	F	F	I	R	E	L	L	I
E	S	A		S	O	X			
			J	A	Y		K	O	A
N	E	W	E	N	G	L	A	N	D
A	B	A	R		B	A	R	E	D
T	A	K	E		I	D	E	A	L
O	Y	E	Z		V	A	N	D	E

20

K	E	P	T	A		J	A	Y	Z
A	X	I	O	M		E	L	I	E
F	U	Q	U	A		N	O	P	E
K	L	U	T	Z	I	N	E	S	S
A	T	E		O	R	Y			
			A	N	A		S	E	P
W	O	R	D	S	Q	U	A	R	E
A	J	A	R		W	H	Y	V	E
W	O	R	E		A	N	N	I	V
A	S	A	P		R	O	O	N	E

21

T	E	S	L	A		D	A	M	S
A	T	T	I	C		A	Q	U	I
K	H	A	K	I		Y	U	T	Z
E	A	S	E	D		D	A	T	E
I	N	H	A	L	E	R			
				S	Y	N	E	R	G	Y
S	P	O	T		Z	A	I	R	E
K	O	K	O		Y	M	C	A	S
I	K	O	N		M	E	A	D	E
P	E	K	E		E	R	N	E	S

22

T	S	K	E	D		O	P	E	D
H	A	N	N	A		N	O	G	O
I	N	E	P	T		E	R	G	O
R	E	E	L	S		S	K	O	R
D	R	S	E	U	S	S			
			I	N	H	E	R	B	S
G	A	R	N		E	N	E	R	O
A	R	E	A		R	I	G	U	P
Z	U	N	I		P	O	A	C	H
A	M	O	R		A	R	L	E	S

23

J	O	S	S		K	M	A	R	T
A	C	T	I		N	O	D	U	H
C	H	E	X		O	P	E	R	A
K	O	W	T	O	W		P	A	N
			W	R	E	S	T	L	E
T	H	R	O	A	T	Y			
Y	A	O		T	H	R	E	E	D
P	L	U	T	O		U	P	T	O
E	L	G	A	R		P	E	N	T
B	E	E	R	S		Y	E	A	H

24

C	H	A	M	P		T	S	A	R
R	O	N	C	O		H	I	R	E
U	N	Z	I	P		E	K	E	S
D	E	A		U	H	W	H	A	T
E	S	C	A	P	E	E			
			M	A	X	B	A	E	R
C	A	N	A	D	A		M	A	E
R	U	I	Z		G	R	A	V	E
A	R	G	O		O	O	Z	E	D
B	A	H	N		N	E	E	D	Y

93

25

I	T	S	O	K	■	H	A	D	J
S	E	I	N	E	■	A	Z	O	O
L	E	N	I	N	■	N	A	N	U
E	T	C	■	W	A	G	N	E	R
T	H	E	G	A	M	E	■	■	■
■	■	S	H	A	M	P	O	O	■
I	M	F	U	L	L	■	O	H	M
T	E	R	I	■	G	A	N	J	A
E	X	I	T	■	A	T	E	O	N
M	I	G	S	■	M	A	R	Y	I

26

P	A	C	O	■	I	N	F	U	N
L	U	A	U	■	T	O	R	R	E
I	N	S	I	D	E	J	O	K	E
E	T	A	■	P	R	I	M	E	D
■	■	B	K	S	■	V	A	L	S
M	A	L	I	■	P	E	T	■	■
A	L	A	S	K	A	■	O	T	B
K	E	N	S	A	L	A	Z	A	R
E	X	C	E	L	■	J	E	D	I
S	P	A	R	E	■	A	D	A	M

27

C	A	T	O	■	B	A	T	C	H
O	T	O	H	■	O	C	H	R	E
P	R	O	M	E	T	H	E	U	S
Y	A	K	■	W	H	E	R	E	S
■	I	M	A	■	B	O	L	O	■
L	A	T	E	■	H	E	Y	■	■
I	T	S	A	G	O	■	A	M	B
M	E	L	L	O	Y	E	L	L	O
I	N	O	I	L	■	T	W	I	X
T	O	W	E	D	■	S	E	X	Y

28

S	L	O	P	S	■	B	A	W	L
H	O	S	E	A	■	A	S	H	E
A	T	K	I	N	S	D	I	E	T
R	S	A	■	D	R	A	F	T	S
P	A	R	T	I	I	I	■	■	■
■	■	H	E	L	M	E	T	S	■
B	O	D	E	G	A	■	D	E	A
Y	O	U	D	O	N	T	S	A	Y
E	Z	R	A	■	K	R	E	M	E
S	E	A	M	■	A	L	L	O	R

29

N	I	M	I	T	Z	■	H	A	J
A	R	E	T	H	A	■	E	C	O
P	A	L	S	U	P	W	I	T	H
■	■	■	A	S	P	I	R	I	N
H	A	I	D	■	A	N	T	O	N
A	T	B	A	T	■	S	O	N	Y
T	H	E	T	R	I	B	■	■	■
F	I	R	E	A	L	A	R	M	S
U	R	I	■	C	I	C	A	D	A
L	D	S	■	T	A	K	E	I	T

30

K	U	R	S	K	■	S	N	A	P
A	K	A	K	A	■	M	A	L	I
P	A	K	I	S	T	A	N	I	S
U	S	E	■	P	E	L	O	T	A
T	E	D	R	A	L	L	■	■	■
■	■	■	I	R	E	L	E	N	T
O	U	T	B	O	X	■	A	I	R
S	T	R	A	V	I	N	S	K	Y
H	E	E	L	■	N	O	O	K	S
A	P	E	D	■	G	U	N	I	T

94

31

```
ICAN  SWIGS
COME  TORAH
BLUEHAWAII
MARTINIQUE
    GNEISS
SAPPHO
TREASURIES
IMPRESSIVE
COSTA  VIES
KRISS  PILE
```

32

```
AMAP  FISTS
REGO  OPART
ANEW  ROWER
LUDWIG  TSO
    OMIGOSH
NEWWAVE
AXE  JEWISH
ICAME  GLEE
LOVER  ALAN
SNEAK  WETS
```

33

```
BREAK  MEHR
JENGA  CLIO
OBJETSDART
REO  MIXTEC
KLYMAXX
    ANTIWAR
BRANDY  ORE
DONQUIXOTE
ALOU  SOLID
YOKE  HOSES
```

34

```
ACQUIT  FAB
ZOUAVE  ALE
ONEEYE  NBA
VEE  TATUM
  NAMEGAME
CDSTORES
LOPEZ  INK
ONA  AMAZON
WNW  RENEGE
NAN  THEDOW
```

35

```
YAP  EMAJOR
OHI  CANUTE
BAZOOKAJOE
  ZONE  YOS
SPAZ  RIFLE
CASES  PRES
ULA  ZASU
BAUDELAIRE
ACCENT  TOY
SEENTO  SHE
```

36

```
SCHWA  OMAS
ALOOF  JAJA
LAKEBAIKAL
SIE  SABERS
AMYL  AWS
  POW  AJAX
AMOSOZ  OLE
CAKEWALKER
EXES  SEENO
HIYA  UNSEX
```

95

37

```
H A R D G   Z A M A
A L E V E   E X E X
Y E S I T   R O D E
D R E   T B O N E S
N O W W H A T
    H I G H L O W
I R T Y S H   E V E
M O O N   D I X I E
U P T O   A P U N K
P E S T   D O S E S
```

38

```
M A S T S   P E S O
A M M A N   A X E S
H A I K U   D T W O
A Z T E C R U I N S
N E H   K H A N
    F U B U   G M A
D A I L Y B R U I N
O X E N   A H I N T
E L L A   R E S E E
R E D S   B A H R S
```

39

```
L A B A N   J P E G
E L U D E   O R A L
G I N Z A   V I S A
U N D E R S E X E D
P E T S I T
        N A R R O W
Z A B A G L I O N E
E R I K   L O U I S
R I G A   E J E C T
O D D S   D A N E S
```

40

```
A D A B   I C A R E
G I R O   R A G E S
H A I R C O L O R S
A M A Z O N   G U I
    O N L Y O N E
B E Z I Q U E
O L A   U N A R M S
O L I V E G R E E N
M I R O S   N A T O
S E E S T   S L A W
```

41

```
S T A K E   S E L L
H O F F A   L E I A
E R I C S T O L T Z
D A R   Y E A S T Y
S H E R M A N
    H A S S L E S
A S P I R E   E D T
T H I N K O F O N E
R E N O   U L N A R
A S K S   T A S S E
```

42

```
S W I T   N A B O O
T E T E   O R A L B
E L S E   W E N D S
A L A D D I N
L O N   R S T U V W
S K O K I E   N I H
    A V E R A G E
B O O Z E   E B O N
A N J O U   A L D A
A E S O P   M E A T
```

96